Tom Dreaper

Tom Dreaper with his head lad, Paddy Murray, in the yard at Greenogue in the 1960's.

Paddy was head lad at Greenogue for some 35 years. The first 25 years for Tom and the remainder for Tom's son Jim.

Tom Dreaper & His Horses

by Bryony Fuller

Introduction by Anne, Duchess of Westminster
Foreword by Sir John Thomson

Punchestown/Marlborough

PUNCHESTOWN BOOKS
Ormond Court, 11 Ormond Quay, Dublin 1

MARLBOROUGH BOOKS
6 Milton Road, Swindon, SN1 5JG
c/o 9 Queen Street, Melbourne 3000, Victoria, Australia

First Published 1991

A limited edition of 75 signed and specially bound copies is published by
The Marlborough Bookshop and Sporting Gallery
6 Kingsbury Street, Marlborough, Wiltshire

Design, Typesetting and Artwork
Typographical Services, High Wycombe, Bucks, England

Printed by Regent Publishing Services Limited
Hong Kong

ISBN 1-873920-00-8 Punchestown
ISBN 1-873919-00-X Marlborough

I first met Mr. Dreaper in 1956, racing at Leopardstown: I introduced myself and said "Would you take a horse for me ?" the answer (thank goodness) was "Yes".

Some years later Tom Dreaper's wife, Betty, told me that when he got home that evening he said "We've got another horse coming" Betty "Good, I hope you liked him", "Haven't seen him", "Do you like the pedigree", "Not much, but I liked the look of the girl".

So began nearly 20 years of the most wonderfully happy friendship and one which continues with Betty and their son, Jim. No words can describe my gratitude to Tom or my admiration for his care and love of horses: that he was the most incredibly successful trainer is well known - 97 winners was his magnificent total for me.

I am indeed proud and very honoured to have been invited to write this introduction.

Anne Westminster

May 1991

AUTHOR'S NOTE

It is now nearly twenty years since Tom Dreaper died, but as he was such a popular and respected figure throughout the chasing world, I had no problems in researching this book. I must have enough material to produce a book in this series of 240 pages rather than 112 or a full length biography.

In fact, since the days of Henry Linde of Eyrefield Lodge on the Curragh, who dominated 'chasing on both sides of the Irish Sea in the 1870's and 1880's, no stable of chasers has ever been as strong as Tom's Greenogue string was during the 1940's, 50's and 60's.

Clearly Tom Dreaper and Henry Linde had two things in common, the ability to get horses to jump well and to select and retain top cross country jockeys.

I have had to leave out photographs not of good horses, but horses verging on the great, which either won at Cheltenham such as Muir and Mountcashel King or the Irish Grand National such as Last Link and Splash, due to pressure of space. I hope by quoting these four horses the reader will understand the quality of horse associated with Tom Dreaper.

AUTHOR'S THANKS

The response for information about Tom Dreaper has been overwhelming and I apologise if I have missed out anyone. Lady Thomson, as Betty Dreaper now is, and her husband Sir John (Breeder/Owner of Fort Leney), have spent many hours helping. Betty's recall for the smallest detail is quite remarkable; where possible I have incorporated her written notes into my text verbatim.

I must thank profusely Sir John and Lady Thomson, Jim and Tricia Dreaper, Michael and Eva Kauntze, and Valerie Dreaper for lending me family albums, framed photographs and press cuttings; I had overkill by at least one hundred per cent. Valerie has been the most tremendous help and kindly had me to stay whilst working on the book. Likewise I must express my thanks for much hospitality to George Ponsonby's widow, Libby, and her son and daughter-in-law (Peter and Faith) who all live at Kilcooley Abbey, and also for large loans of material for the book.

Anne, Duchess of Westminster has taken immense trouble throughout the book's production, as has her secretary Anne Stubbs. I am not only very grateful for their help but would like to express particular thanks to the Duchess for writing the Introduction.

Sir John Thomson kindly wrote the Foreword; Tom trained winners of the Cheltenham Gold Cup for both the Duchess and Sir John so it is especially fitting that they are both associated with this tribute to him.

Tim Cox has done sterling work in researching Tom's records, which I am passing on to the family for posterity.

I hope that individuals will realise for brevity I have left out any Army titles and awards.

Pat Taaffe, Toss Taaffe, Paddy Mullins, Paddy Sleator, Bunny Cox, Tim Hyde, Aubrey Brabazon, Edward O'Grady, George and Elsie Wells, Dick Francis, Ken Oliver, Jack White, Eddie Brennan, Mrs Hussey and her staff at Ashbourne House Hotel, Alison and Dodo Baker, Cecil Ronaldson, Felicity Wilson, Roy Craigie and Norman Colfer and their staff at Fairyhouse Racecourse, Joan Moore and the Masters of the Kildare Foxhounds and their staff at Punchestown Racecourse, Baron Martin de Roebeck, Frank O'Reilly, Mona and Jonny Croome-Carol, Frank and Rachel Le Hane, John Welcome, Reg Green (Mr. Grand National), Raymond Smith, Michael O'Farrell, The Clerks of the Courses of Leopardstown Racecourse, Aintree Racecourse and Cheltenham Racecourse, Valentine Lamb and his ever helpful staff at The Irish Field, The Masters of the Tipperary Foxhounds, Jeannine Alexander, Sarah Chidgey, Rupert Collens and finally but not least members of The Irish Turf Club and The I.N.H.S.Committee and their staff on the Curragh.

Foreword

I am delighted that a book has been written about Tom Dreaper. He became a close friend after first training for me over 30 years ago. Since then, Tom and his son Jim have trained a hundred winners for me at Greenogue to date. I am now lucky enough to be married to Tom's widow, Betty.

It is a great privilege to be asked to contribute this foreword as Tom was undoubtedly one of the greatest trainers of steeplechasers in the sport's long history.

He trained for many friends of mine, some of them London Bankers. Like nearly all Tom's owners they were in steeplechasing for the sport. Tom once remarked that he had been led to believe that Bankers were sensible prudent people and yet he trained for no less than six of them!

Tom never had any ambition to train a large string of horses. He felt that he could only know about 35 horses really intimately and he also wanted plenty of time for his other interests.

When J.V. Rank invited him to go over to England as his private trainer, Tom thanked him but said that he was born in County Meath and that was where he wanted to spend his life. J.V. Rank replied, "Alright then, I will have my horses in Meath."

Tom described himself as primarily a farmer, and he was renowned as a wonderful judge of stock. When he stayed with us in Scotland he was never happier than when walking out to the hill and patiently watching the cattle as they grazed.

He was an excellent host and we all enjoyed the dinner parties he and Betty gave at Greenogue. He liked to go to bed reasonably early. One evening when it was getting late, a fellow guest remarked to me, "It's the first time Tom hasn't asked me by this time whether I hadn't a home to go to!"

He was a wonderful employer. His skilled and loyal staff remained with him over the years and many of them are still with Jim at Greenogue.

Tom was a regular churchgoer but he always walked out before the sermon. This did not in the least annoy or insult the clergyman who had the greatest respect and admiration for Tom. When Tom died, St. Patrick's Cathedral in Dublin was filled with a congregation from all walks of life in Ireland; and many more from England.

James and Harriet Dreaper.
These photographs were taken around 1910 at Donaghmore House, County Meath.

1890 – 1919
SCHOOL AND FARMING YEARS

In the 1890's James and Harriet Dreaper were substantial farmers on the County Meath/County Dublin borders, living at Donaghmore House, near Ashbourne. In England they would have been described as prosperous hunting yeoman.

They were to have four children: Richard (Dick) born in 1896, Thomas William (Tom) born in 1898, Pansy born in 1900 and some five years later, Connie.

The Dreapers were Irish Protestants and Tom was a staunch church-goer all his long life. Although, in later years, he was often seen to slip out before the sermon, he would never conclude any business deal on a Sunday.

Just before Tom's fifth birthday, on the 28th September, he attended school for the first time when he joined his brother Dick at the National School in Ashbourne. Ashbourne is perhaps better known as the home of the Ward Union Staghounds than for its educational institutions. At the age of twelve, Tom once again followed his brother Dick when he went as a boarder to St Andrew's College, Dublin. Tom left no lasting impression there academically, either in the Army Cadet Forces, which in pre-first World War days was compulsory, or on the playing fields. He actively disliked football and although he didn't shine academically, or as an athlete, his contemporaries remembered him affectionately as a quiet and amusing companion who always did enough work to keep well out of trouble. He was renowned for his droll sense of humour throughout his life and by the time he was forty had become equally famous for his 'quotations'.

Donaghmore is only ten or fifteen miles, as the crow flies, from the heart of Dublin and it wasn't until the mid 1960's that the urban spread in any way affected rural pastimes. It was heaven in those far off days for the Dreaper children, who loved the ponies and horses which their parents supplied in abundance. In winter there was hunting with the Ward Union Staghounds, Meath Foxhounds and Fingall Harriers, all of whom met within hacking distance of the family home. In the Spring and Summer holidays there were point-to-points, race meetings, gymkhanas and, of course, the great Dublin Show, held every August.

Tom's parents had no involvement whatsoever with racing, whether at point-to-points or at proper licenced meetings, although it must be said his Mother was a McKeever, and the McKeevers have produced generations of fine amateur and professional jockeys. It is perhaps from this distaff line that Tom acquired his passion for racing or, to be more precise, chasing.

In 1916 he left school and joined his Father and elder brother working on the increasingly prosperous family farms. In winter there was always enough time and horses to hunt at least two days a week. However, Tom was besotted with thoroughbreds and racing and, given half a chance, used to play truant from the family business to ride work for any one in the vicinity who would let him gallop or school point-to-pointers or, even better, proper racehorses.

The Dreaper children -
Tom, Richard (Dick), Pansy and Connie - around 1910.

Mrs Dreaper, Connie, Jackie Carpenter, Pansy and Tom.

Tom holds his sister, Pansy's pony.

St. Andrew's College, Dublin, 1915. Tom is sitting, middle row, third from left.

St. Andrew's College, Dublin, 1915. Tom is the boy in the foreground.

Connie

Pansy

Mrs. Dreaper

The Dreapers not only hunted but also played tennis and croquet.
The pictures on these two pages are from the early 1920's.

Dick, Mr. Morrison and Tom with his dogs.

The early 1920's were troubled times for Eire with the Civil War; blowing up bridges was a favourite pastime. These photographs come from Betty Dreaper's family album.

Betty Dreaper (then Elizabeth Eva Russell) aged about three and ten on her donkey.
Betty, like Tom, came from a hunting family.

Tom on his first Point-to-Point winner Dean Swift at the Fingall Harriers Point-to-Point on 6th March 1923.
Tom leads the field on his own Copper Top in the Ward Union 'Red Coat' Members Race around 1930.

1920 – 1938
THE RIDING YEARS

The years 1918 to 1923 were more problematical for Irish racing than the years 1914 to 1918. Ireland was torn apart by a combination of Civil War, political unrest and strikes which resulted in many race meetings being abandoned. For instance, the entire Punchestown meeting had to be cancelled in both 1919 and 1920, the only occasions since 1865, with the exception of 1882, the meeting had not been held. The Irish Grand National meeting was also cancelled in 1919.

It is therefore not surprising that our budding hero did not ride his first winner between the flags at a point-to-point, until he was well into his twenties. By the time he was thirty, Tom had developed into one of Eire's finest riders of point-to-pointers and hunter chasers. The majority of these races were run over courses which included banks, sometimes an open ditch, and quite often a stone wall, as well as brush fences. Horsemanship as opposed to jockeyship was at a premium.

The early 1930's saw two developments in Tom's life which proved crucial. In 1930 his parents purchased a 300 acre farm two miles from Donaghmore House, called Greenogue, and he went to farm there on his own account. Greenogue, like the Walwyn's Saxon House, or the Rimell's Kinnersley Stables, over the next forty years, became a legendary name in National Hunt circles. In 1931 Tom took out a public licence for the first time.

In the early years at Greenogue, he had relatively few horses and they were of marginal, economic importance. It must be said that Tom always regarded himself as a County Meath cattle and sheep farmer first and foremost. Even after he had won Cheltenham Gold Cups and Irish Grand Nationals, he always tried to take each Wednesday off from his horses, when possible, to attend to his cattle business at Dublin market with his brother Dick, until it closed in the 1960's.

Tom had no formal education in racing stables, rather the reverse: he graduated from his family's yard of hunters via point-to-pointers to training proper. He therefore developed his own unique system based on a normal hunting yard routine. Traditionally, in a racing stable the staff arrive at around 7 a.m. The first lot, approximately half of the horses in the yard, go out at around 7.30 a.m. and return an hour or an hour and a half later; the lads have breakfast and the second lot go out at around 11 a.m. The horses are then groomed and fed and the staff leave at lunchtime returning only for evening stables at around 4 p.m.

Tom's routine, which he never changed until he retired in the 1970's was very much his own. The staff arrived around 8.30 a.m. and the horses started going out in two's or three's at 9 a.m. It was very seldom that any horse was out of its stable for more than 45 minutes. The staff had their lunch in the tack room, groomed their horses between 2 p.m. and 4 p.m. and went home at 4.30 p.m.

The horses received four feeds a day, breakfast before the lads arrived at 7.30 a.m., lunch at around 12.30-1 p.m., tea at around 4 – 4.30 p.m. and dinner at around 8 p.m. Betty, when discussing Tom's routine with me, put great emphasis on the four feeds a day that Tom insisted upon rather than two or three which is usual in other stables. The Head Man did the feeding.

Paddy Mullins, a top class pilot himself in his younger days, and now Eire's leading National Hunt trainer, who rode against Tom in point-to-points in the 1930's said, "When I was just starting off, Tom and Paddy Sleator were the tops. You always expected one of them to be riding the favourite in any point-to-point, even down the country in Wexford or Waterford."

Tom in his late twenties.

Tom's career as a top amateur rider came virtually to a halt in 1938 after a particularly successful Fairyhouse and Punchestown when his horse went through the wings in a hunter chase at Naas, after which he spent eight weeks in hospital, two of them unconscious. Tom rode a few winners after this, the most notable being a 'chase at Down Royal, on 12th March 1939, on a horse called 'Ultimatum'. This was the day the news that Hitler's armies had marched into Austria reached Eire. He also rode Prince Regent when he won his first race in 1940.

TOM DREAPER'S RIDING RECORD AT FAIRYHOUSE AND PUNCHESTOWN

1929	wins 1	rides 3
1930	wins 1	rides 7
1931	wins 4	rides 8 (a)
1932	wins 0	rides 3
1933	wins 0	rides 2
1934	wins 0	rides 3
1935	wins 2	rides 6 (b)
1936	wins 1	rides 5
1937	wins 0	rides 0
1938	wins 3	rides 7 (c)

(a) Won Prince of Wales Plate and La Touche
(b) Won Prince of Wales Plate
(c) Second in Irish Grand National and won Prince of Wales Plate

From left: Mr. P. J. Lenehan, Mr. L. T. Byrne, Mr. J. M. Morrison, Mr. H. Kenny, jun., Mr. F. Clark, Tom, Mr. E. Mc Keever and Sir. E. Goff.
Behind: Mr. J. B. Rogers, Mr. W. J. Hilliard and Lord Fingall.

Tom and other leading amateur riders in 1931.
This was the first year he took out a public licence to train.
He worked hard to better the lot of trainers in Ireland and was a founding member of the Irish Trainers' Association.

Tom in 1936, on his way to victory at Punchestown on Brave Edna.

Tom on My Branch (partly covered) in the 1938 Irish Grand National in which he was second.
This was Tom's last year as a serious amateur rider. It was also the last year The Grand National was run over a course which included banks.

The 1940's were the most important decade of Tom's life he married Betty and trained Prince Regent.

1939 – 1949
MARRIAGE AND THE PRINCE

The 1940's were the most important decade of Tom's life. He married Elizabeth (Betty) Russell and trained the mighty Prince Regent.

Prince Regent was described by the most sporting of sporting artists, Snaffles, as "The dream horse" and it would be fair to say that Tom not only enjoyed training the wonderful horse but, more importantly, his marriage to Betty proved the greatest success and they were to be blissfully happy together for some thirty years. Betty became a vital member of the Greenogue stable. Toms masterly handling of The Prince drew leading owners attention to his ability as a trainer of top class horses.

In the first ten years of Tom's training career, up to the outbreak of the Second World War, jump races run in Eire were primarily aimed at producing young horses of ability to go over to be trained in England. Schooling young horses for English owners and dealing for most Irish trainers, including Tom, was as important as the training of winners. It wasn't until well into the 1950's that Tom stopped dealing. He was a brilliant judge of all stock, including cattle, so was able to select potential National Hunt horses, and show hunters in the rough, and also bought and sold the odd made hunter.

It must be remembered that in the 1940's Tom had less than twenty stables and during the 1950's and 1960's these were slowly increased until he could stable nearly thirty-five horses.

As an amateur rider Tom had excelled at Ireland's two biggest steeplechase meetings at Fairyhouse and Punchestown and as the forties developed his intention to train top class horses to run at top class meetings came to fruition. There was no pot hunting for the Dreaper horses round the smaller country tracks. They ran well at the major tracks or, if they couldn't win there, were quickly sold.

A very large majority of the horses Tom trained came to him as green, untried, three or four year olds. Now, if they were good enough, they remained with him throughout their racing career. His ability to pick suitable horses and then nurture them can perhaps best be explained by statistics. Using the annual *Horses-in-Training* book as a basis, I estimate that between 1946 and 1970 Tom had some 326 horses through the stable - including the thirty or so that he handed over to Jim. They won 749 races out of a total of 3012 runs, which gave him a strike rate of over 21%. It must also be emphasised that of these 749 winners, twenty-six were at the National Hunt Festival and another ten were in Ireland's greatest chase, the Irish Grand National.

Tom was primarily a stockman and instinctively knew exactly how to handle cattle, sheep, and young horses. He was particularly famous for the heavy Hereford cross bullocks which his prime County Meath land produced annually. He had a great affinity with cattle and when the pressure of training in his later years became intense, he would go out and look at them. This gave him an inner calm which was to prove one of his tremendous strengths. No trainer since Tom's day has ever taken so many good horses with a favourite's chance to Cheltenham, and the pressure must have been considerable.

Tom took considerable trouble selecting the young horses he trained and would give those with ability as much time as they needed. If necessary he would keep them for two or three years before they had a run in public. He was as careful at selecting his owners as he was his young horses. First and foremost, his owners had to be in the game for fun. Tom regarded racing as a sport and not as an industry. Although he wasn't anti-betting, there was no question of laying horses out for easy races before a gamble. As I have already noted, his horses won over 20% of the races in which they ran, and although I have not calculated the exact figure, I would estimate that they were in the first four seventy or eighty per cent of the time; proof that they were always out to do their best.

Tom always set himself personally the highest of standards and expected his staff and horses to perform well at all times. Behind his courteous and charming manner, Tom had the determination and will of iron necessary to succeed at anything he set his heart to. By the time he got married, his cattle and sheep were some of the best in Ireland. The few horses he chose to show at Dublin were normally in the top two or three of their class, and having tasted fame with 'The Prince', he was now determined to continue winning races on both sides of the Irish Sea at the highest level.

In Tom's yard there was no shouting, bad temper or rudeness from the boss; so common in many National Hunt yards, especially as tension builds up before the great Spring meetings at Cheltenham, Liverpool, Fairyhouse and Punchestown. However, beneath Tom's humorous and calm exterior lay more than a hint of steel. In fact some people would go as far as to say that at times he was a bit of a martinet. Tom brought out the best in everyone working with his horses and many of his staff remained at Greenogue for decades rather than years. Although Tom is remembered with great affection, especially by those close to him whether his lads, jockeys or owners, he certainly did not suffer fools gladly, a not uncommon trait amongst top trainers and one which he shared with both Fred Winter and Fulke Walwyn.

Tom was a genius when it came to dealing with animals and a perfectionist and it is impossible to pin point exactly what made him so successful. The jumping ability of his horses undoubtedly played a very important part. As soon as a young horse was broken, and Tom believed in plenty of long reining with a caveson and surcingle when breaking, or as soon as they arrived, Tom got his youngsters jumping. He often had them jumping before they had a man on their back and definitely before they went fast.

The country around Greenogue is ditch country and the youngsters were introduced to jumping over open ditches. Tom had the young horse bridled and put on a caveson with a long rope. He was led up to the edge of an open ditch where he was held and allowed to have a good look into and across the ditch. The man holding the horse threw the rope across the ditch to a couple of lads waiting in the landing field. The horse was encouraged to bring his hind legs up to his front legs and then made to jump the open ditch from a stand, using his hocks to produce propulsion. After he had repeated this a few times, the horse did it quite calmly and walked up to the edge, settled himself and took off.

The next stage in the horse's education was over baby bush fences where he was lunged around and around jumping the fences slowly in each direction. Only when the horse was jumping open ditches and bush fences sensibly using his hocks properly, was he ridden over fences.

Horses were never allowed onto the gallops until they could jump cleanly. As soon as the young horse was broken and jumping properly, he was turned away until the Fingall Harriers started hunting.

It was a well known sight to see Tom on a made horse leading six, seven or more youngsters backwards and forwards over the North County Dublin and Meath ditches, not always in the direction hounds were moving. Fortunately the Fingall Harriers were hunted by the Craigie family who often had horses, such as Fortria, Splash and Last Link, all bred by them at Greenogue, all of whom were Irish Grand National winners, so they were sympathetic.

As the years went on and young chasers became more expensive, owners did not like to risk them being hunted, but Tom often said that he never had one badly damaged. Early Mist, a Grand National winner never managed to master the art of jumping from a standstill but that didn't stop him from running well many times at Liverpool.

PRINCE REGENT

The tale of how Tom Dreaper came to have The Prince is a tragic one. As a three year old he was sent by his owner's, Mr. J.V. Rank, racing manager, Harry Bonner, to be broken and educated in Cork by the young Vet Bobby Power. Bobby was killed soon afterwards when changing a punctured wheel on his car, and The Prince was sent to Greenogue where Tom took over his education including hunting him with the Fingall Harriers. As a four year old, in the spring of 1939, he went to Mr. Rank's private estalishment on Salisbury Plain to be trained by Gwyn Evans, and like Bobby, he was soon killed in a car accident. Prince Regent was then sent back to Tom to be trained.

Prince Regent did not appear on a racecourse until he was five and in March and April 1940 he ran in three bumpers ridden by Tom winning on his last appearance at Naas. Still backward, the next season he was once again restricted to three runs, winning a couple of nice races at Phoenix Park and Dundalk. By the summer of 1941, he had developed into a tremendous individual, and was clearly a horse of great potential.

By now steeplechasing had ceased in England due to The War and so a whole generation of Irish chasers remained in Eire to compete against each other for remarkably small prizes, quite often The Prince had to run in races worth well under £100 to the winner.

In the 1941/42 season he won five of his seven races including the Irish Grand National under 12st. 7lbs; in the 1942/43 season he won three of his six races and was second under 12st. 7lbs in the Irish Grand National. In the 1943/44 season he won one of his four races and was once again second in the Irish Grand National under his usual top weight.

By the time chasing had started again towards the end of the War Prince Regent was two and a half stone or three stone ahead of other chasers in Ireland. He was unable to make an appearance in the 1945 running of the Cheltenham Gold Cup as a warble appeared near his withers.

The 1945/46 season was to confirm The Prince as the only chaser that could then be compared to Golden Miller. He made his first appearance in England at Wetherby on 15th December 1945 when at the prohibitive odds of 10 to 1 on he won The Bradford chase. The race was worth £100 to the winner and Tom had sent The Prince over mainly for a school over the stiffer English fences and to let him have a look at a water jump as there were none in Ireland at that time.

On 14th March he made his only appearance in the Cheltenham Gold Cup. The Prince was now eleven and so great was his reputation that he started four to seven on favourite. Not since the clash of Golden Miller and Thomond in the 1933 Gold Cup had any chase, with the exception of the Grand National, caused so much excitement. Long before the horses appeared in the parade ring it was surrounded ten deep by a knowledgeable crowd waiting to see the Irish Hero. Undoubtedly the best looking horse in training on either side of the Irish Sea, the English public, like the Irish public, took The Prince immediately to their hearts. He won most convincingly as an odds on favourite should do.

Tim Hyde his regular jockey realised in the race that age was creeping up fast on The Prince and said to Tom the immortal words, "It took me a minute or two to beat that fellow today". Clearly the writing was on the wall for The Prince and few Englishmen were to see him at his greatest.

After his Gold Cup victory he ran a tremendous race under 12st. 5lbs. to be third in the Liverpool Grand National starting three to one favourite, given reasonable luck he would have won. The following season he won The Champion Chase at Liverpool in November and carrying 12st. 7lbs. starting eight to one favourite for the National itself, finishing fourth.

Prince Regent winning the Irish Grand National in 1942, carrying 12st 7lbs

Prince Regent's owner J.V. Rank, jockey Tim Hyde and trainer Tom in a rather sombre mood at Leopardstown in 1946.

BALDOYLE STEEPLECHASE. FEBRUARY 12TH 1944.

First time round; Erinox leading from Golden Jack, Prince Regent, Barghora, Prince Blackthorne, and The Clip.

BALDOYLE STEEPLECHASE. FEBRUARY 12TH 1944.

Second time round; Erinox still leading followed by Prince Blackthorne, Golden Jack, Prince Regent, Barghora, Ruby Loch, Summer Star, Knights Crest, and Mountain Loch.

BALDOYLE STEEPLECHASE. FEBRUARY 12TH 1944.

The battle of the Princes is over. Prince Blackthorne having fallen at the last leaves Prince Regent to win easily by eight lengths from Ruby Loch with Knights Crest third.

BALDOYLE STEEPLECHASE. FEBRUARY 12TH 1944.

Tim Hyde rides The Prince into the unsaddling enclosure after one of his most meritorious victories. Although he won easily it was a tremendous battle for the last mile until Prince Blackthrone departed at the last.

Prince Regent, aged 10, jumps the water before winning at Wetherby in December 1945.
He was Tom's first runner in England.
This was the first time the Prince had seen a water jump, as there were none in Eire.

Prince Regent winning the Cheltenham Gold Cup in 1946 from Poor Flame. A few days later he ran a magnificent race to be third in the Liverpool Grand National and the following year he was fourth.
He won a Champion and a Bechers Chase over the big fences at Liverpool in 1946 and 1947 respectively.

The Wedding

St. Patrick's Cathedral, Dublin,
19th June 1945.

Betty's Aunt and Uncle, Jim and Jennie Goodbody

Gertrude Goodbody arrives with the bride's mother Eva Russell

The Wedding

St. Patrick's Cathedral, Dublin,
19th June 1945.

Tim Hyde, Danny Morgan, Tom, Dick, Frank Sutherland and Noel McClancey (Tom's assistant trainer).

The Wedding

St. Patrick's Cathedral, Dublin,
19th June 1945.

Tom's sister Pansy, now Mrs. Cannon, arrives with her daughter Sheila

Mrs. Mary Baker, the breeder of Arkle, poses with her two daughters, Alison and Dodo.

A large crowd of well wishers including "card sellers" help the Bride and Bridegroom into their car.

A Great Hunt with the Wards

31 December 1943

by

Pansy Cannon

Oh boys! but that hunt was a wonderful sight,
Why, the pack wasn't home til nine-thirty that night.
They started from Nutstown, where Con had the hind,
He knew for some days it was there she reclined.
When they met they were seventy odd I am told.
Eleven 'twas finished - and they were stone cold.

The pace began hot, and grew faster and faster -
No riding on hounds - not a word from the Master.
At Ashbourne our Vet was next door to a fall,
With great presence of mind he grabbed at the wall.
His horse had slipped up and twisted a shoe,
Poor Harry was finished - what more could he do?

In a fence by the Bush road so narrow and deep
Sheila Lyons' horse was stuck there in a heap.
No efforts could move him, he just wouldn't try
But a lorry with ropes pulled him out bye and bye.
As we crossed at the Poorhouse, young Cooney - poor chap,
Got a fall off the road and then lost his check cap.

Near Pelletstown Covert we met a 'Quare' fence -
A Tarzan-like jungle, so thick and so dense.
The Dairyman broke through the branches a track,
And Dermot got through with the twigs swinging back.
He left as momento his best shining topper
But anything's better than coming a cropper.

Culmullen came next and I saw Leonard's cattle
Stampede for the road like chargers in battle.
They jumped a stone wall and fell out on the road -
It's as well he's a sport or he'd surely explode.
For later that day - Oh Master! - Tut-Tut!
The wire on his avenue somebody cut.

Young Ivan was game and so was his horse,
Tho' we'd like to have heard Tom Dreaper's discourse.
For the horse was so beat that at Barry's he stayed,
While Ivan was home in a motor conveyed.
By now it was evening, with light growing dim,
The hind had us beaten, we had to give in.

When at Ferrans we finished, that field of eleven,
We spoke to the Master and said: 'It was Heaven.'
He gathered his hounds and midst the hub-bub
I heard him say smiling: 'Now where's the first pub?'
And a boy on a bike said: 'A pub is it, boss?
You'll find one down further at Garadice Cross.'

As I drank at the pub I was gazing around,
Two Mangans were there, and three Craigies I found,
Nora Parr and Lance Smith - he's from far Donabate
And the Dairyman too - his last fence was a gate.
Harkie Collen thought all should go home by a bus,
'Your horse can be led' said the Craigies 'by us'.

We'd a rest at the Hatchet and drank and ate sweets,
And talked of the Wards and their wonderful feats,
And when we moved off - was the Dairyman tight?
For I know that he said to a signpost 'Goodnight.'
He and I had to turn at the K gates for home,
So I know nothing more - that's the end of my poem.

The Dairyman was Frank Cannon, Tom's brother-in-law,
The Vet was Henry O'Leary.

Tom poses with the ageing Prince Regent on the Greenogue gallops during the 1947/1948 season.

Tom borrows Betty's hunter, Drinagh, for a day with the Wards during the 1948/1949 season.

Keep Faith owned, like Prince Regent, by J V Rank winning the 1946 Galway Plate
for Tom and Tim Hyde.

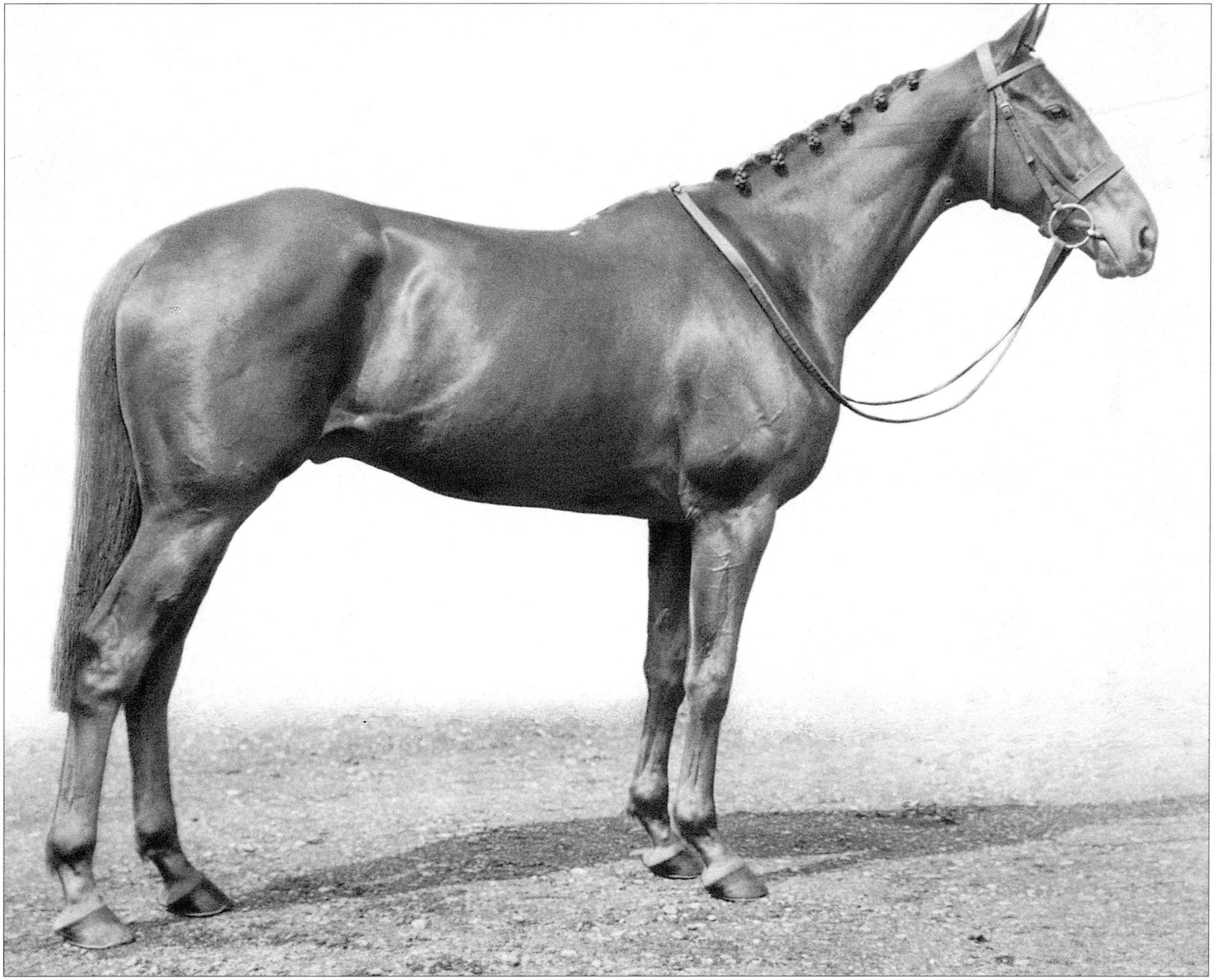

A posed portrait of Keep Faith, a typical Dreaper horse. The majority were beautifully built and proportioned, had a bold outlook, a kind eye, and were up to plenty of weight. The horses owned by his most successful owners such as Jimmy Rank, Lord Bicester and Anne, Duchess of Westminster, were normally the best looking in the paddock and with very few exceptions they could gallop and jump.

Greenogue in the mid 1940's with Timmy Hyde walking up to the gallops.

Insert: Storm Head winning at Leopardstown in 1949 ridden by Pat Taaffe. He became one of the best chasers in England when trained by Charlie Hall in Yorkshire.
Martin Molony riding Hasty Bits to win the 1950 Conyingham Cup at Punchestown, together with the Galway Plate, the second most important chase in the Irish Racing Calendar after the Grand National.

Shagreen winning the 1949 Irish Grand National for Jimmy Rank ridden by E. Newman. Newman was Tom's stable jockey, between Hyde and Taaffe.

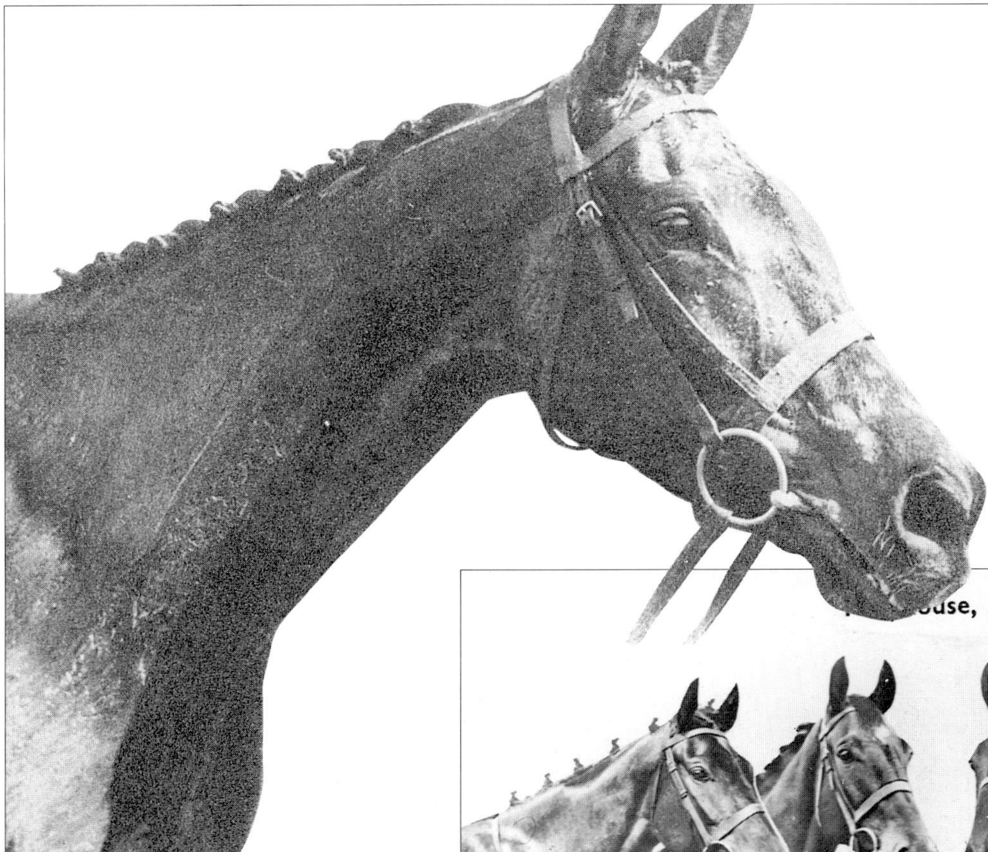

Tom won three other good races at Fairyhouse in 1949 and the little card shown above was produced to commemorate the event as one had been in 1942 for the Prince's Irish Grand National win. Tom was now recognised as the greatest trainer of chasers Ireland has produced in the twentieth century, and he was only in his early fifties.

A beautiful jump by Shagreen ridden by the young Pat on the way to victory in the Johnstown Handicap Chase at Leopardstown in October 1952 carrying 12 st. 10lbs.
Tom asked Arkle to carry the same weight at Cheltenham in the Massey Ferguson, when he finished third, the only time he was ever beaten at Cheltenham.

Shagreen wins the Sutton Hurdle, at Baldoyle at 20 to 1 to give Jimmy Rank a nice pay day from the bookmakers. Although Tom's was essentially a non betting stable, and Mr. Rank's vast number of National Hunt and Flat horses and coursing greyhounds were run entirely openly this didn't mean that Mr. Rank wasn't willing to have a tilt at the ring. Shagreen was put in this hurdle race to try and sharpen him as he had become slightly disinterested with fences. He had already won an Irish Grand National and a Bechers Chase at Liverpool. Jimmy thought that 20 to 1 about such a high class horse was ridiculous and he always said that Shagreen's win that day was one of his most enjoyable.

Bright Cherry wins at Baldoyle in September 1950. Seven years later she became the dam of the immortal Arkle.

THE 1950'S EXPANDING

If there was any doubt that after Prince Regent faded from the scene Tom was to be a major training force, it was quickly dispelled at the Fairyhouse Easter Meeting in 1949. He won four chases, including the Irish Grand National with Shagreen.

In the 1940's and 1950's Tom had two main patrons J. V. Rank, who owned Prince Regent and Shagreen, and Lord Bicester who had some very useful horses with him, but nothing quite the quality of Rank's best.

In early 1952 Jimmy Rank died and his horses ran on in his widow's colours for the rest of the season, before being sold at auction in Derby week. Tom lost two top class horses in this sale. Clifford Nicholson purchased Stormhead who won some top chases, when trained in the North of England, while Vincent O'Brien purchased Early Mist for 'Mincemeat' Joe Griffin, with Lord Bicester the underbidder. Early Mist won the 1953 Grand National ridden by Bryan Marshall.

Aintree's Grand National, on which I shall comment later, was certainly an unlucky race for Tom and most of his patrons, except for Anne, Duchess of Westminster who won it with a horse trained by Captain Tim Forster.

Jimmy Rank was second in the 1937 Grand National with Cooleen and unluckily third with Prince Regent in 1946. Perhaps if he had lived another year he may have won with Early Mist. Lord Bicester was second in the 1949 Grand National with Roimond and maybe one more wave of his catalogue at the Rank disposal sale would have given him a winner in 1953 with Early Mist. Tom trained Roimond as a young horse but never Cooleen.

Tom and Betty's family was completed a few months after Early Mist won the Grand National, with the arrival of their third child Valerie in October. She joined a sister, Eva born in January 1949 and a brother Jim born in January 1951. Valerie tells me that Tom was a devoted and attentive Father, although rather stern. It isn't really surprising that he should appear a little bit stern occasionally, as he was well over fifty when Eva was born.

In 1956 the Dreaper's Man o' War was supreme champion at the Dublin Show and after this huge success, Tom did little more dealing. Each child from quite an early age had his or her own pony.

Lord Bicester and Tom, although they may have been unlucky over Early Mist, were rewarded with perhaps the most able horse to run in chases either in Eire or England in the 1950's. Royal Approach, an all quality very dark brown gelding, won a bumper as a four year old on the 27th December 1952 at Leopardstown and pulled out seven days later to win a maiden hurdle at Naas, just a few days after his fifth birthday.

In the next season, 1953/54, Royal Approach set the racing world alight when he won six races on the trot, five of these over fences. He won the Cathcart at Cheltenham's National Hunt Festival meeting and then, still only six, won the Irish Grand National under 12st., starting as even money favourite. As Royal Approach returned to Greenogue after his Grand National win, he was being talked of as another Golden Miller or Prince Regent. However, tragedy struck within days when Royal Approach was injured out at grass. An attempt was made to bring him back after a two year rest but he was only a shadow of his former self.

Royal Approach at the last fence first time round in the Irish Grand National which he won in 1954. Royal Approach won all his races that season - six in total including the Cathcart Chase at the Cheltenham National Hunt Festival. Royal Approach looked like he could have been another Prince Regent but, within days of his National victory he was injured in a paddock and was never the same horse again.

Lord Bicester receiving the trophy from Mrs. O'Reilly after the Irish Grand National. Lord Bicester's horses were always tremendous individuals. When I asked Dick Francis at the 1991 Grand National what type of horse he liked to ride in the race, he said "One of Lord Bicester's lovely great chasers like Finnure who helped to make the fences look small".

Betty and the children, Summer 1954.

Tom and the children in the river, Summer 1955.

Eva and Valerie ride Goldie, Tom and Jim on his beloved Patch, Summer 1956.

Tom and Jim at a gymkhana at Prospect Hill in 1958.

Betty on their lovely show hunter Man O' War who was Supreme Champion at the Dublin Show in 1956.

ENTER THE DUCHESS

Prince Regent was many people's dream horse and within a few years of his retirement and the much mourned death of Jimmy Rank, two other shining stars were to come to Greenogue.

It would be fair to say that the Duchess of Westminster, who approached Tom in the 1950's to train for her, was every trainers' dream owner and with the possible exception of H.M. The Queen Mother she has become the most popular owner ever of chasers and one of the best Ambassadors of the Sport.

Nancy, as she is known to her friends, had everything a trainer required of an owner; she was married to one of the richest men in the world, who died soon after her association with the Greenogue stable, but even more important in racing than money is luck and certainly the Duchess has had plenty of that in the last thirty years or so.

Perhaps she has made her own luck as she has been responsible for selecting many of her own horses including the immortal Arkle, the second star. The Duchess is in the game for fun, loves her horses and they seem to respond by giving their best for her.

Born in Cork she was brought up with animals and became a fine horsewoman, and as I comment on page 109 of the book, she has a great affinity with all animals.

I think the table to the right of this page demonstrates both her and Tom's ability with chasers.

It is perhaps worth noting that Tom became the greatest of friends with both Jimmy Rank and Anne, Duchess of Westminster (to address her by her correct title nowadays), and they both enjoyed a very special relationship with this quite remarkable man.

DUCHESS OF WESTMINSTER'S HORSES TRAINED BY T.W.D.

	1st	2nd	3rd
Arkle	27	2	3
Badna Bay	-	2	-
Ben Stack	10	4	2
Buca di Bacco	2	3	3
Cashel View	8	2	2
Foinavon	3	2	5
Fortinbras	-	-	2
Gala Day	1	1	1
Garrynagree	7	3	-
Geordie Hugh	2	-	-
Highland Pique	-	2	-
Meall Horn	1	-	1
Pine Marten	1	-	-
Reay Forest	2	2	2
Saville More	-	-	-
Sea Brief	7	1	1
Sentina	2	4	2
Suirvale	3	7	2
Ten Up	4	1	1
Tinkers Green	-	1	-
Tubbercosh	4	-	1
Twigairy	4	4	3
Vulmore	1	-	-
Willow King	6	2	2
	97	43	33

Tom's first big winner for the Duchess was Cashel View in the 1959 Galway Hurdle.
The Duchess was to put a black band on her colours after her husband's death hence the variation between Cashel View's and Arkle's colours.

A nice double for the resolute partnership of Tom Dreaper and Pat Taaffe at Manchester in November 1956 with the bay Dizzy winning the Emblem Chase by 12 lengths and the grey Rose's Quarter winning the Pathfinder Chase by 10 lengths.

Betty and the family at Killarney in the summer of 1960. "The wettest day there ever was".

Tom's staff in mid winter during the season 1967/68.

THE 1960'S
VIRTUALLY UNBEATABLE

There have been many great trainers in the history of National Hunt Racing on both sides of the Irish Sea. Some have trained important winners over a long period and others have done tremendously well for a season or two. Tom's record in the 1960's is unique and in the limited amount of space for text in this book, I am going to let the statistics do the talking again.

First, let us consider Tom's record at Cheltenham's National Hunt Festival. The Blue Ribband of chasing is the Cheltenham Gold Cup run over an extended three miles, and the most important race for fast chasers is The Queen Mother Two Mile Champion Chase. The major test for novices the Sun Alliance Novices Chase for future Gold Cup horses run over three miles, and the test for the fast novice horses is the Arkle Challenge Trophy, run over two miles. Set out below are Tom's winners in these races in the sixties. The reader must remember that his horses had been running well there since 1946. No-one has and no-one is likely to match this record for training and producing great chasers at Cheltenham, for many people the place that really matters.

The Cheltenham Gold Cup - four times
1964, 1965, 1966 and 1968.
The Queen Mother Two Mile Champion Chase - five times
1960, 1961, 1964, 1966, 1969 (and 1970).
The Sun Alliance (The Broadway Novice Chase and Tote Champion Novices Chase) - twice
1963, 1965 (and 1970).
The Arkle Challenge Trophy (The Cotswold Chase) - twice
1961, 1963 (and 1971).

In Ireland his winning record in top chases was perhaps even more spectacular and obviously the Irish Grand National is the most important race. I have selected a couple more at random to emphasise my point.

The Irish Grand National - seven times
1960, 1961, 1962, 1963, 1964, 1965 and 1966.
The Leopardstown Handicap Chase - seven times
1962, 1963, 1964, 1965, 1966, 1967 and 1968.
The Thyestes Handicap Chase - four times
1962, 1964, 1965 and 1966.

With two exceptions all the 1960's winners at the Cheltenham Festival were ridden by Pat Taaffe.

I have discussed Tom's handling of Arkle, Fortria and Flyingbolt, all superb horses of the 1960's, separately. Tom's handling of the Fortina gelding, Fort Leney, also demonstrated his uncanny ability. In the Totalisator Novices Chase at Cheltenham in 1964 as a six year old Fort Leney had the most tremendous battle with Buona Notte and went down by half a length. His owner, Colonel John Thomson, said as his horse was led in that he assumed that was the end for the season, but Tom replied, "No, he will win the Power Gold Cup at Fairyhouse and the Jameson Gold Cup at Punchestown." Fort Leney went in on both occasions, as Arkle had the previous season.

Tom knew exactly what he could ask a young horse to do without damaging his courage, for Fort Leney continued to race in top class quality company for a number of seasons. In 1968 Fort Leney gave Tom his fifth victory in the Cheltenham Gold Cup, (his fourth in the 1960's), when he was led over the last by The Laird, but fought back like a tiger up the hill to win by a neck.

Lord Donoughmore's outstanding mare Olympia winning the 1960 Irish Grand National ridden by Toss Taaffe.

Right – Olympia, ridden by the owner's son, The Hon. Mark Hely-Hutchinson, circles at the start before winning a chase at Cheltenham's November 1960 meeting.

Another winner at Cheltenham's November 1960 meeting was George Ansley's Fortria seen here winning the Mackeson Gold Cup; a race he was to win again in 1962.

Fortria wins the National Hunt 2 Mile champion chase at Cheltenham's 1961 Festival - the race is now named after Her Majesty, The Queen Mother.

FORTRIA

Fortria was a typical high class Dreaper horse. He was bred in 1952 by Tom's neighbour, Alec Craigie out of his mare Senria who Tom had trained in the 40's to win a number of races. His sire was Fortina a French bred horse who had won the 1947 Cheltenham Gold Cup as a six year old. Tom trained a large number of Fortina's progeny with great success, including winning the Irish Grand National four times with four different offspring. Tom found most very able but quirky, however, Tom's ability and patience with that type of horse was limitless.

Fortria raced for seven seasons winning 20 races, two hurdle races and eighteen chases. He was particularly effective at Cheltenham and his record there says it all:-

1958	NH Festival - Cotswold Chase - won
1960	NH Festival - NH 2M Champion Chase - won
1960	November - Mackeson Gold Cup - won
1961	NH Festival - NH 2M Champion Chase - won
1961	November - Mackeson Gold Cup - second
1962	NH Festival - Cheltenham Gold Cup - second
1962	November - Mackeson Gold Cup - won
1963	NH Festival - Cheltenham Gold Cup - second

Amongst other major races won by this top class and durable servant of Greenogue was the 1959 Pathfinder Chase at Manchester, the 1961 Irish Grand National and the 1962 Hermitage Chase at Newbury. In all the races mentioned here Fortria was ridden by Pat Taaffe.

Fortria was a very fast horse and like many Fortina's didn't quite get the Gold Cup Trip at Cheltenham, although Tom won the Cheltenham Gold Cup in 1968 with one of his offspring, Fort Leney. Glencaraig Lady, also sired by Fortria, won a Gold Cup but she would have been more effective at Cheltenham at slightly under three miles.

Kerfero, ridden by Liam McLoughlin, leads at the last to win the Irish Grand National in 1962 from the Dan Moore trained Team Spirit. Tom also won the Irish Grand National in 1963 and 1965 with Last Link and Splash belonging to Alec Craigie. The Craigie family like the Dreapers have been stalwarts of hunting in the area covered by the Fingall Harriers, Meath Foxhounds and Ward Staghounds and were associated with the Greenogue stable for many years. Team Spirit won the Liverpool Grand National in 1964 when trained by Fulke Walwyn

Mr. F. Stafford's tough mare Kerfero winning the 1962 Thyestes Chase ridden by Liam McLoughlin from Brown Diamond. Tom was to win the Thyestes four times in the 1960s. Unlike many top National Hunt trainers, Tom's stable normally contained a few mares many of which won important races for him.

In really bad weather Tom's horses exercised on the Strand at Portmarnock, fifteen miles from Greenogue. This picture was taken during the terrible winter of 1962/63. Olympia leads Badna Bay, Stormy Flight and Pine Martin.

Above – An equally happy Tom at Leopardstown after Fort Leney won on 1st February 1964; behind Tom is Fort Leney's owner. That day Flyingbolt won the Scalp Hurdle and Arkle the Leopardstown Chase.

Right – A happy Tom flanked to his left by Tom Taaffe, the father of Pat and Toss and to his right the great racing administrator Seamus McGrath, taken in the 1940's.

Fort Leney winning his maiden hurdle at Naas in December 1963. Ridden by Pat he is seen jumping the last alongside Our Joy ridden by Mr. E.J. Cash. Fort Leney was bred and owned throughout his career by Col. John Thomson now Sir John Thomson.

The actor, Gregory Peck's Owen's Sedge wins the 1963 Leopardstown Chase. Betty described Gregory to me as "The nicest man you could ever meet."

Three of the greatest judges of young chasers at Goff's Sale then held at Ballsbridge in Dublin. Harry Bonner, who bought Prince Regent for J.V. Rank, Anne, Duchess of Westminster who selected Arkle herself and purchased him at these sales and Tom.

ARKLE AND FLYINGBOLT

In the 1960's Greenogue was to be home to two very different but great horses Arkle and Flyingbolt. Arkle was bred on the traditional chasing lines favoured by Tom who had trained his dam, Bright Cherry, and ridden his grand-dam, Greenogue Princess, while Flyingbolt's pedigree was more suited to the flat.

I asked Alison Baker, whose Mother bred Arkle, see page 38 for a photograph of them at Tom and Betty's Wedding, what made Arkle so very special and she simply replied "he was very intelligent." There can be no doubt that there has never been a better chaser than Arkle. My research has led me to believe that in his heart of hearts Tom would always rank The Prince as Arkle's equal.

Arkle's story is rightly covered in a book devoted to him by Ivor Herbert, so all I now intend to do is justify my statement that there was never a better chaser. Arkle made his debut over fences on the 17th November, 1962 in the Honeybourne Chase at Cheltenham which he won, including this race he ran 26 times over fences, winning 22. Of his 22 victories three were in the Cheltenham Gold Cup and he won the 1964 race by five lengths, the 1965 race by twenty lengths and the 1966 race by thirty lengths. In the 1964 and 1965 Cheltenham Gold Cup the second horse was Mill House, also foaled in 1957 like Arkle, and who had won the 1963 Cheltenham Gold Cup by 12 lengths from the Dreaper trained Fortria. Mill House prior to the 1964 Cheltenham Gold Cup was talked of as a rival to Golden Miller and Prince Regent, but Arkle was clearly superior.

Arkle was the nearest thing ever to a racing machine over fences and I would like to deal with his four defeats out of his 26 races. His first defeat came in the 1963 Hennessy Gold cup at Newbury when carrying 11st 9lb compared to Mill House under 12st when he ran third. It is generally conceded that his defeat that day was brought about by hitting a piece of false ground after jumping the last open ditch in the straight, although the race would have undoubtedly been close. His second defeat over fences came in December 1964, when he found carrying 12st. 10lb. too much in the Massey-Ferguson at Cheltenham. Tom was to remark to Michael O'Farrell of the *Irish Times* before this race 'Weight will even stop a train.' His third defeat came when trying to give Stalbridge Colonist almost two and a half stone in the Hennessy in 1966 and his final defeat was on December 27, 1966 when he injured himself in running during the King George VI Chase at Kempton which resulted in his retirement. I don't think that any chaser including Golden Miller and Prince Regent had a better record.

I also asked Alison Baker what made Tom so special and she replied in her usual straightforward manner two things, "We always knew him as a high class trainer of high class horses and he was dead straight."

The other really great horse Tom had in the 1960's was the flashy chestnut Flyingbolt. He was a very different proposition to Arkle. In the 1963/64 season he proved himself by far the best hurdler Tom trained when he was fluent winner of the Scalp Hurdle in February, and then won a division of the Gloucester Hurdle at the Cheltenham National Hunt Festival Meeting. The next season 1964/65 he won five 'chases on the trot including the Cotswold Chase at the Festival Meeting. The 1965/66 season was to be his most successful he ran eight times, six over fences and twice over hurdles. He won all of his six 'chases including the Two Mile Champion Chase at Cheltenham and the Irish Grand National. Having won the Two Mile Champion Chase at Cheltenham he was to run a blinding race to be third in the Champion Hurdle. Alas after that season he went wrong and it would be unfair to judge him on his subsequent races.

One must ask oneself the question how good was Flyingbolt - certainly he lacked one of the main attributes of every chaser which is durability. Over two or two and a half miles it is doubtful that there has ever been a better chaser and he was certainly Arkle's equal if not superior up to two and a half miles, but over three or three and a half miles Arkle would have been much the better horse.

Arkle winning the Broadway Chase at Cheltenham's National Hunt Festival in 1963. Arkle's great rival Mill House, also a six year old, won the Gold Cup that year.

Arkle returned from Cheltenham to put up two more very promising performances that Spring. Firstly he won the Power Gold Cup at Fairyhouse and then the Jamieson Gold Cup at Punchestown, see insert.

Arkle started off the 1963/64 season by winning his only flat race in October. He is seen romping home in the Donoughmore Flat Race at Navan ridden by T.P. Burns. Later that month he won the Carey's Cottage Chase at Gowran Park but was beaten by Mill House in the Hennessy Gold Cup at Newbury in November.

The Gold Cup at Cheltenham's National Hunt Festival saw the clash of the giants when the previous year's winner Mill House was challenged by Arkle, who won impressively. Here Pat and Arkle lead the beaten Mill House and Willie Robinson.

I asked the Duchess what she thought was the greatest of all of Arkle's victories and she replied,. "The first Cheltenham Gold Cup when he beat Mill House; it was so exciting."

Flyingbolt with his distinctive white blaze and Arkle lead Tom's string round a field.

In the winter, Arkle walks up to the gallops over the river. In the summer, when Tom's children were tiny he used to play with them in this river just below the bridge. See page 54.

The Duchess leads Arkle in after winning the 1964 Hennessy Gold Cup at Newbury. He carried 12st 7lbs that day and started 5 to 4 favourite. By now he was becoming the hero of the English as well as the Irish racing public.

Arkle carrying 12st 7lbs and starting at 4 to 9 on well over the last to win the Whitbread Gold Cup at Sandown in April 1965. This convincing victory over 3m 5f under top weight clearly stamped Arkle as an all time great along with Golden Miller and Prince Regent. A few weeks earlier he had won his second Gold Cup at the Cheltenham National Hunt Festival.

248 **T. W. DREAPER, Kilsallaghan**

Kilsallaghan, Co. Dublin, Ireland.
Postal: **Greenogue, Kilsallaghan, Co. Dublin, Ireland.**
'Phone: **Dunboyne 250187.**

1 **ALPHEUS**, 4, b g Valerullah—Olympia
2 **AMPHIBIAN**, 5, ch m Zarathustra—Olympia
3 **MEALL HORN**, 8, b g Archive—Stylo
4 **SAVILLE MORE**, 6, ch g Fortina—Headwave
5 **TWIGAIRY**, 6, b g Prefairy—Twigina
6 B g, 4, Vulgan—Fortlass
7 **GARRYNAGREE**, 6, br g Neron—June the Fourth
8 **DROPIT**, 5, b or br g Seminole II—Letgo
9 **BLACK LAD**, 5, b g Black Tarquin—Moyle Lady
10 **STRAIGHT FORT**, 6, b g Straight Deal—Fortlass
11 **COLEBRIDGE**, 5, b g Vulgan—Cherry Bud
12 **FULL PLUME**, 7, br g Coxcomb—Kind Approach
13 **LEAP FROG**, 5, b g Trouville—Maggie's Leap
14 **NOBSKA**, 4, b g Duplex—Rocky Light
15 **RONAN**, 10, ch g Bowsprit—Nas na Riogh
16 **FORT BRIDE**, 4, ch g Fortina—Colines Bride
17 **ROUGH SILK**, 6, b g Black Tarquin—Flossie
18 **CROWN PRINCE**, 9, br g Pendragon—Arab Lady
19 **EAST BOUND**, 5, ch g Arctic Slave—Jari Pataka
20 **EXPLOSION**, 5, b g Brilliant Pil—Naughty Nancy
21 **FARM LODGE**, 6, ch g Snow King—Queen's Approach
22 Ch g, 5, Fortina—Nicolaus' Dream
23 **FORT LENEY**, 11, b g Fortina—Leney Princess
24 **PROUD TARQUIN**, 6, br g Black Tarquin—Leney Princess
25 **PRINCE TINO**, 10, br g Fortina—Leney Princess
26 **LIMESTONE CASTLE**, 6, br g Black Tarquin—Sand Castle
27 **MUIR**, 10, ch g Snow King—Metra
28 **TACKLER'S PRIDE**, 5, b g Seminole II—Tackler
29 **BLACK SECRET**, 5, b g Black Tarquin—Secret Pact
30 **STONEDALE**, 6, b g Duplex—Rocky Light
31 **VULTURE**, 7, b g Vulgan—Cherry Bud

THREE-YEAR-OLDS

32 **COMEA**, b f Little Buskins—The Grange
33 **NATA** (U.S.A.), ch f Atan—Little Notice

Owners : The Earl of Donoughmore, Her Grace Anne, Duchess of Westminster, Mrs R Whineray, George Ansley, Gen R K Mellon, **Major G T** Ponsonby, Col and Mrs T G Wilkinson, Col and Mrs John Thomson, Mrs Jean E Bowman, Jack Bamber, O Vanlandeghem, C Nicholson, W Willis, A Craigie, J T R Dreaper, Mrs T W Dreaper.

Jockeys : Pat Taaffe (10–5), Liam McLoughlin (11–0), **Patrick** Woods (9–10), Sean Barker (9–5), Peter McLoughlin (9–8), Wm McCabe (9–8), Patrick Collins (10–8), Ed Wright (9–2). **Amateurs** : Mr J T R Dreaper (9–7), Mr Val O'Brien (10–8)

1714 COTSWOLD CHASE £1,365 2m & few yds 2.15 (2.17)
1671* **FLYINGBOLT** 6-12-4 PTaaffe hit 4th: hdwy 9th: led last: r.o—1
1283 Princeful 7-11-8 KBWhite stdy hdwy fr 9th: unable qckn flat 5.2
1588* Ballinaclasha 8-12-1 PPickford hit 8th: led 2 out: blnd last: r.o one pce 4.3
1652 Final Approach 7-11-5‡7 RBarry no hdwy fr 10th nk.4
1556 Tibidabo 5-11-4 Nicholson h: nvr nrr 8.5
1595² Eastern Harvest 8-11-8 SMellor no hdwy fr 8th 15.6
1551³ Ringside 7-11-8 TBiddlecombe in rear fr 5th 7
1560 Acrophel 6-11-8 Scudamore led 6th tl fell 10th 0
1660 Prince of Ormonde 7-12-1 JMorrissey led to 5th: 4th whn fell 10th 0
Deetease 7-11-8 EPHarty bhd whn p.u bef 10th 0
1565 Solabra 6-12-1 ...GScott prom tl brt dwn 9th 0
1538* Selworthy 6-12-4 RVibert mid div whn brt dwn 9th: destroyd 0
1556* Jaxartes 7-12-1 ...PJones uns rdr 1st 0
S.P.: 4/9 FLYINGBOLT (2/5—40/85), 10 Tibidabo(op8/1), 100/8 Selworthy(op8/1), 100/7 Solabra(op100/8), 20 Ringside,Acrophel, 25 FinalApproach, 33 Ors. Tote 6/2: 6/2 76/8 22/8. Mrs T G Wilkinson (T Dreaper, in Ireland) 13 Rn 4m 3.2

1723 CHELTENHAM GOLD CUP (Chase) **£7986 10s 4 5 (4.10)**
abt 3m 2f 76y
1670* **ARKLE** 8-12-0 ...PTaaffe j.w: mde all: qcknd appr last: v easily ....—1
1487* Mill House 8-12-0 GRobinson hit 16th: ev ch whn pckd 19th: hrd rdn 2 out: one pce ...20.2
Stoney Crossing 7-12-0 MrWRoycroft j.w: no ch fr 19th 30.3
Caduval 10-12-0 OMcNally a.wl bhd bad.4
S.P.: 30/100 ARKLE (2/7—1/3), 100/30 MillHouse(tch 7/2), 33 Caduval(op25/1), 100 StoneyCrossing(op200/1,blow). Tote: 5 - (5/8). Anne, Duchess of Westminster (T Dreaper, in Ireland) 4 Rn 6m 41.2

1895 SANDOWN, Sat., Apr. 24th (Good) (CBT)
(Other races under Jockey Club Rules)

2208 WHITBREAD GOLD CUP £8,230 3m 5f 18y 3.10 (3.11)
(H'cap Chase)
1723* **ARKLE** 8-12-7 ...PTaaffe j.w: hit 4th: led to 16th: led 21st: qcknd flat ....—1
1994* Brasher 9-10-0 (7x) JFitzGerald led 17th to 20th: one pce fr 21st 5.2
2143 Willow King 10-9-7 Mellor hdwy 16th: nvr nrr 20.3

595

2.0—Bradford Chase. £100 ; 3m.
228² Prince Regent 10-12-6 T Hyde 1
270² Gyppo 11-11-5* Mr J Cousins 2
289 Gaudy Knight 11-11-3 F Maxwell 3
257⁴ Troymint 12-11-3 R Burford (fell)
Vendor II 9-11-3 A Thompson (pulled up)
S.P.: 10 on PRINCE REGENT, 20 others.
Tote: 2/3. Places : 2/1, 2/1.
½l, dist. In IRELAND. (MR J V RANK.)

THE FIELD HUNTING YEAR BOOK

FINGAL

Kennels—Kileek, St. Margaret's, Co. Dublin. Stations : Dublin or Malahide.
Couple of Hounds—15. Height 20 in.
Masters—Alexander Craigie, Esq. ; Richard Collen, Esq.
Secretary—Robert Craigie, Esq., Harristown, St. Margaret's, Co. Dublin.
Huntsman—Michael Grant.
Whipper in—Tony Grant.
Hunt Uniform—Green and gold.
Subscription—£5 5s. non-landholders. £3 3s. landholders in the district. Cap, ladies and gentlemen 10/– each.
Hunting Days—Tuesdays and Fridays.

RESULTS AT POINT-TO-POINT MEETING

HELD AT MOORETOWN SWORDS ON FEBRUARY 26th.

LIGHT-WEIGHT RACE.—Mrs. N. J. Kelly's GREENOGUE PRINCESS (Mr. T. W. Dreaper), 1 ; Mr. R. Dreaper's ARGILLACEOUS (Owner), 2 ; Mr. S. H. Lynch's LUKEWARM (Mr. D. A. Moore), 3. Five ran. Won by three lengths ; a bad third.

LADIES' RACE.—Miss Joan Manley's NATIONAL HUNT (Owner), 1 ; Mrs. R. Craigie's BELLVERO (Miss P. Morgan Byrne), 2 ; Miss B. Sherlock's M.C. (Mrs. Henry), 3. Four ran. Won by six lengths ; a length separated second and third.

LIGHT-WEIGHT RACE.—Mr. S. H. Lynch's DORYAN (Mr. T. W. Dreaper), 1 ; Mr. J. Farrell's PRINCESS CHERE (Mr. Reynolds), 2 ; Mr. M. J. O'H. Macardle's OLD SPINSTER (Owner), 3. Seven ran. Won by a distance ; a neck separated second and third.

HEAVY-WEIGHT RACE.—Mr. J. Farrell's IRISH BREEZE (Mr. A. G. N. Reynolds), 1 ; Mr. H. O'Leary's WEE WILLIE III (Capt. Corry), 2 ; Mr. F. Rogers's BENIGHTED (Mr. F. Lillingston), 3. Six ran. Won by a head ; four lengths separated second and third.

FARMERS' RACE.—Mr. J. J. Ryan's EAGER BETTY (Mr. T. W. Dreaper), 1 ; Mr. J. Cox's TUBBERHONAN STAR (Mr. P. Woods), 2 ; Mr. J. Farrell's DARK BRIDE (Mr. A. G. N. Reynolds), 3. Six ran. Won by three-quarters of a length ; five lengths separated second and third.

Betty, with the Basset Hound Laurel, and Tom, with the Dachshund Zulu, relax for the press photographers at Greenogue at the height of Arkle's fame. It is very unusual to find a photograph of Tom without a hat or his pipe.

The most popular horse since 1946, Arkle parades to raise money for the local football club next to Greenogue. Pat looks decidedly apprehensive.

Pat looks very much happier as he wins the Donkey Derby.

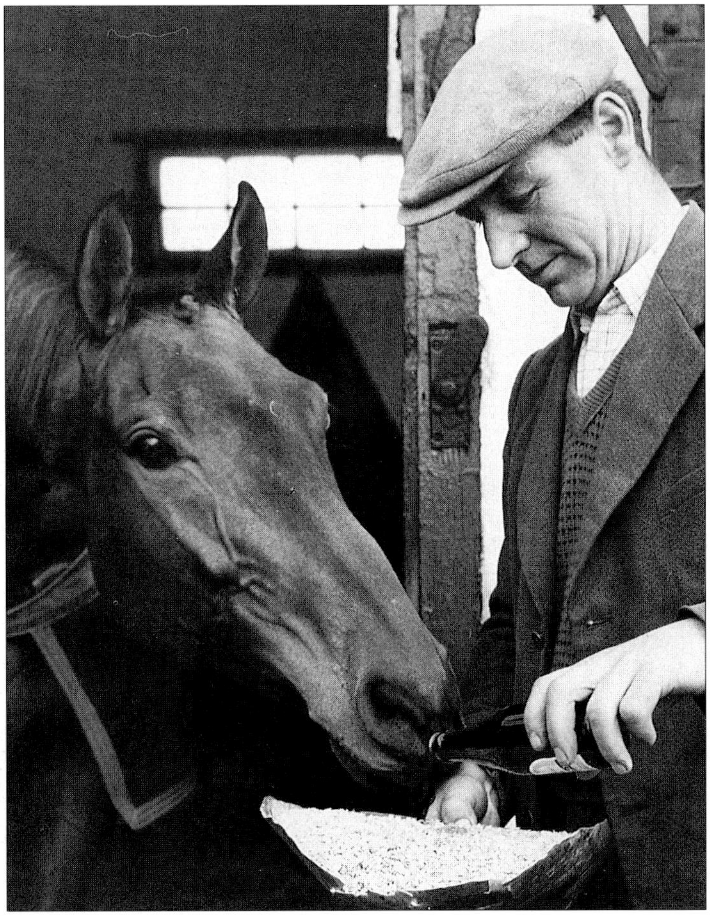

Arkle gets his lunch dampened down with a bottle of Guinness from Paddy Murray.

Valerie shows Arkle her pet lamb.

A great study of Arkle and Pat on the way to winning the King George VI Chase at Kempton on 27th December 1965. The following March he won his third Cheltenham Gold Cup off the reel.

Tom had plenty of other top class horses in his stable during the Arkle era. Perhaps the best looking horse ever to grace the Greenogue stables was the Duchess's Ben Stack, seen here jumping the last to win the Cotswold chase at Cheltenham's National Hunt Festival in 1963, the same year as Arkle won the Broadway Chase. Ben Stack also won the Two Mile Champion Chase at the Festival in 1965.

Arkloin jumping the last in the National Hunt Handicap Chase at the 1966 Cheltenham Festival under 12st 5lbs on the way to an easy victory. Arkloin was by the same sire as Arkle, Archive. Like so many of the great horses which Tom and his son Jim were to train at Greenogue he came from George and Libby Ponsonby's Kilcooley Abbey.

Flyingbolt ridden like most of the horses in this part of the book by Pat Taaffe jumps a hurdle on the way to victory in the Scalp Hurdle at Leopardstown in 1964. He was Tom's best hurdler and won the Gloucester Hurdle at Cheltenham's National Hunt Festival in 1964 and was unlucky in running when third in the 1966 Champion Hurdle, the day before he'd won a chase at the Festival.

Flyingbolt jumping a fence second before winning the Black and White Gold Cup Novice Chase at Ascot in December 1965 on the way to an impressive win. As well as being a top class hurdler Flyingbolt developed into a really fine chaser.

Counter Charge, owned by Mr. Charles Haughey, was another very useful winner for Tom in the 1960's.

Stonehaven, ridden by Ben Hanbury, now the successful Newmarket trainer, winning at Sandown in 1960's when trained by R. Armytage but had been introduced to racing from Greenogue.

Tom and Jim after their first ride at Phoenix Park on Ribble in March 1967 when they finished fourth. Like his Father, Jim became a highly proficient and brave amateur and again following in his Father's footsteps he has sent out a number of great winners from Greenogue including the Irish Grand National four times, The Gold Cup and The Queen Mother Champion Chase at Cheltenham.

Fort Leney ran a great race to be second in the Totalisator Novice Champion Chase in 1964 at the Cheltenham National Hunt Festival and then came back to emulate Arkle by winning the Power Gold Cup at Fairyhouse and the Jamieson Gold Cup at Punchestown, see insert.

The second fence in the 1968 Cheltenham Gold Cup - Pat Taaffe on Fort Leney; Terry Biddlecombe on Stalbridge Colonist and Jeff King on The Laird. The Laird led Fort Leney over the last but at the line Fort Leney was half a length to the good to give Tom his fifth Gold Cup.

Tom and Pat had three winners at the 1970 National Hunt Festival at Cheltenham. Straight Fort, left, won the Champion Two Mile Chase and Proud Tarquin, a half brother to Fort Leney, won the Totalisator Champion Novices Chase. Their third winner was Garrynagree in the Cathcart.

THE 1970'S
THE LAST WINNERS AND RETIREMENT

Very few trainers manage to keep a powerful string of horses for thirty years, but the quality of horses Tom had in his stable on the 1st January, 1970 was as good, if not better, than throughout the 1950's and 1960's. By the turn of the decade he was well past seventy, but with the long-established support of Betty, and increasing help from Jim, his son, the stable was as dangerous in 1970 and 1971 as it had ever been.

Tom's final two years as a trainer got off to a brilliant start at the 1970 Cheltenham National Hunt Festival, when two of the four big chases went to the Greenogue stable. Straight Fort won the Queen Mother Two Mile Champion Chase and Fort Leney's half brother, Proud Tarquin, won the Sun Alliance Chase. Garrynagree made it a treble by winning the Cathcart.

Jim (Dreaper) was now riding with tremendous dash and maturity and in November, 1970 landed the Troytown Chase at Naas on his God-Mother's, Mrs. J Watney, Black Secret.

The 1971 Cheltenham National Hunt Festival came around and once again Tom's horses were to the fore. Alpheus put up a superb performance under E. Wright, having jumped the last well down to storm up the hill to win the Arkle Challenge Trophy giving him his twenty-sixth winner at the National Hunt Festival.

Black Secret was allotted 11st. 5lbs. in Aintree's Grand National and, ridden by Jim, was strongly fancied at 20 to 1. Five horses came to the last with a chance: Sandy Sprite, Bowgeeno, Black Secret and Astbury and behind them Specify. Jim and Black Secret forged ahead. With 100 yards to go it looked as though at long last the Dreaper National jinx was to be laid to rest, but with just a few strides to go John Cook forced Specify to relegate Black Secret to second.

The 1971/72 season was to be Tom's last, but the winners continued to flow in major chases in both Eire and England. In December he handed over his licence to Jim, who has kept the Greenogue colours well to the fore in major chases since. Jim has already trained four Irish Grand National winners, the same number as Paddy Mullins, and they are both joint second to Tom's record of ten winners.

Tom and Betty built a cottage on the farm at Greenogue and Tom retired to his cattle and sheep, respected by everyone in racing and loved by those who had the privilege of knowing him. Tom died in April, 1975 and his funeral at St. Patrick's Cathedral, Dublin, was crowded by people from all walks of life, not only racing and farming.

I would like to finish off my text on Tom by quoting two of his retorts for which he was so famous:
Hurst Park;
David Gibson, a steward at the meeting about Pat Taaffe;
"Are you satisfied with your jockey?"
Tom's reply, "I have worse at home".
Goff's Sales - Looking at young horses;
Maxie Crosgrove, the famous horse vet, "Tom, buy him and give him time."
Tom's reply, "Time, look what it's done for you and me".

In March 1970 Betty and Tom's eldest daughter, Eva, married Michael Kauntze. They now train top class flat race horses at Bullstown, once part of The Greenogue farm.
Left, Michael, Eve with the page David Spillane, Tom with the bridesmaid Tracy Piggott and Lester Piggott.

Carol Watney, Jim's Godmother and owner of Black Secret

Tom and Betty.

Mr and Mrs Charles Haughey
with Diana Craigie.

Jim wins the Troytown Chase at Navan in November 1970 on Black Secret from Miss Hunter. Jim and Black Secret were only just beaten in the 1971 Liverpool Grand National by Specify.

THE ENGLISH GRAND NATIONAL

Luck is a funny thing and Tom was certainly lucky to train so many winners at Cheltenham, Fairyhouse and Punchestown. However, the run of play went against him at Aintree.

In most runnings of Liverpool's great race Prince Regent would have carried 12st. 5lbs. to victory in 1946. He was left in front well over a mile out with a whole load of loose horses around him, and Tim Hyde had to keep riding finishes to get in front of them so that he wasn't baulked at each fence. Tim having to keep pressing the accelerator so often meant that the great horse's engine, finally ran out of petrol after the last, and he was run out of victory by lightweights.

Although Prince Regent was beaten into third place in 1946 his performance that day is recognised to be one of the most magnificent ever put up around Liverpool before the fences were modified. Certainly the handicapper thought so as he was asked to carry 12st. 7lbs. the following year and although well past his best ran into fourth place. The three horses in front of him all carried under 11 stone.

In the summer of 1952 Tom lost Early Mist, at Jimmy Rank's dispersal sale, a few months before he was to win at Liverpool in March 1953. He was then trained by Vincent O'Brien who was to win the following year with Royal Tan and a third time on the trot, in 1955, with Quare Times who was ridden by Tom's stable jockey Pat Taaffe. Pat also won the race again in 1970 on the Fred Rimell trained Gay Trip. Foinavon, also passed through Tom's hands, before he was the fluke winner in 1967.

In 1970 Vulture, owned by General Mellon and ridden by S Barker, was second but he never really looked a winner in the last mile or so. The next year, the last in which Tom had a runner in the National, Black Secret ridden by his son Jim took the lead after the last fence to be pipped near the post and beaten a neck by Specify.

THE IRISH GRAND NATIONAL

Tom was second as an amateur rider in the 1938 Irish Grand National, a few weeks before his horrific fall at Naas which virtually ended his riding career. If the run of play went against him at Aintree on the whole it was very much in his favour at Fairyhouse, the home of the Irish Grand National.

Tom trained his first winner of Ireland's most important chase on the 6th April, 1942 when the mighty Prince Regent carried Tim Hyde and 12st. 7lbs. to victory in a race worth £745. In the next two runnings of the race, always carrying 12st. 7lbs. The Prince was second.

Tom's next winner came in 1949 with Shagreen. Perhaps the confirmation of Tom as an all time great trainer came in the 1954 running of the Irish Grand National when the six year old, Royal Approach, carrying 12 stone and starting even money favourite, won his sixth race of the season.

The 1960's record of Tom's achievements in the Irish Grand National is incredible - he won the race seven times on the trot. His winners were: 1960, Olympia; 1961, Fortria; 1962, Keforo; 1963, Last Link; 1964, Arkle; 1965, Splash; 1966, Flyingbolt.

His record of ten victories achieved between 1942 and 1966 with a string of never more than thirty-five horses is unlikely to be beaten. The handicapper by the late 1940's never did the Greenogue horses any favours and Tom's horses often carried top weight in Eire's greatest chase either to victory or a place.

Fairyhouse racecourse is the nearest course to Donaghmore and Greenogue. Tom had a very special relationship with it, he would have hunted over it with the Ward Staghounds long before he actually rode there as an amateur. He was very successful there as an amateur rider, see page 20 for his record, and not only trained the winner of the Irish Grand National ten times but all the other big races regularly.

Alpheus, ridden by E. Wright, jumps the last a good length down from Veuve before winning the Arkle Trophy at the 1971 National Hunt Festival at Cheltenham.

This was Tom's last winner at the Festival and a suitable finale as this was the fourth time he had won this race which was previously called the Cotswold Chase. His other winners were Fortria, Mountcashel King and Ben Stack.

Cheltenham's National Hunt Festival

GOLD CUP

1946	**Prince Regent**	**T. W. Dreaper**	**T. Hyde**
1948	Cottage Rake	M. V. O'Brien	A. Brabazon
1949	Cottage Rake	M. V. O'Brien	A. Brabazon
1950	Cottage Rake	M. V. O'Brien	A. Brabazon
1953	Knock Hard	M. V. O'Brien	T. Molony
1959	Roddy Owen	D. Morgan	H. Beasley
1964	**Arkle**	**T. W. Dreaper**	**P. Taaffe**
1965	**Arkle**	**T. W. Dreaper**	**P. Taaffe**
1966	**Arkle**	**T. W. Dreaper**	**P. Taaffe**
1968	**Fort Leney**	**T. W. Dreaper**	**P. Taaffe**
1970	L'Escargot	D. L. Moore	T. Carberry
1971	L'Escargot	D. L. Moore	T. Carberry

WATERFORD CRYSTAL CHAMPION HURDLE

1946	Distel	C. A. Rogers	R. J. O'Ryan
1949	Hatton's Grace	M. V. O'Brien	A. Brabazon
1950	Hatton's Grace	M. V. O'Brien	A. Brabazon
1951	Hatton's Grace	M. V. O'Brien	T. Moloney
1960	Another Flash	P. Sleator	H. Beasley
1963	Winning Fair	G. Spencer	Mr.A. Lillingston

QUEEN MOTHER TWO-MILES CHAMPION CHASE

1959	Quita Que	D. L. Moore	Mr. J. R. Cox
1960	**Fortria**	**T. W. Dreaper**	**P. Taaffe**
1961	**Fortria**	**T. W. Dreaper**	**P. Taaffe**
1964	**Ben Stack**	**T. W. Dreaper**	**P. Taaffe**
1966	**Flyingbolt**	**T. W. Dreaper**	**P. Taaffe**
1969	**Muir**	**T. W. Dreaper**	**B. Hannon**
1970	**Straight Fort**	**T. W. Dreaper**	**P. Taaffe**

NATIONAL HUNT CHASE

1949	Castledermot	M. V. O'Brien	Lord Mildway
1953	Pontage	D. L. Moore	Mr. J. R. Cox
1954	Quare Times	M. V. O'Brien	Mr. J. R. Cox
1964	Dorimont	T. Taaffe	Mr. C. Vaughan

GLOUCESTERSHIRE HURDLE

1952	Cockatoo	M. V. O'Brien	Mr. A. S. O'Brien
1953	Assynt	D. J. Morgan	E. Newman
1954	Stroller	M. V. O'Brien	P. Taaffe
1955			
Div. 1	Vindore	M. V. O'Brien	Mr. A. S. O'Brien
Div.11	Illyric	M. V. O'Brien	T.P. Burns
1956			
Div. 1	Boy's Hurragh	M. V. O'Brien	Mr. A. S. O'Brien
Div.11	Pelargos	M. V. O'Brien	Mr. A. S. O'Brien
1957			
Div.11	Saffron Tartan	M. V. O'Brien	T.P. Burns
1958			
Div. 1	Admiral Stuart	M. V. O'Brien	T.P. Burns
Div.11	Prudent King	M. V. O'Brien	T.P. Burns
1959			
Div 1.	York Fair	M. V. O'Brien	T.P. Burns
Div.11	Albergo	C. Magnier	D. Page
1962			
Div. 1	Tripacer	D. L. Moore	T. Carberry
Div.11	Clerical Grey	P. Murphy	G.W. Robinson
1964			
Div. 1	**Flyingbolt**	**T.W. Dreaper**	**P. Taaffe**
1965			
Div.11	Havago	P. Sleator	H. Beasley
1968	L'Escargot	D. L. Moore	T. Carberry
1970			
Div. 1	Ballywilliam Boy	P. Sleator	R. Coonan

CATHCART CUP

1954	**Royal Approach**	**T. W. Dreaper**	**P. Taaffe**
1958	Quita Que	D. L. Moore	Mr. J.R. Cox
1961	Quita Que	D. L. Moore	G.W. Robinson
1965	Scottish Memories	P. Sleator	H. Beasley
1966	Flying Wild	D. L. Moore	T. Carberry
1968	**Muir**	**T.W. Dreaper**	**P. Taaffe**
1969	Kinlock Brae	W.T. O'Grady	T.E. Hyde
1970	Garrynagree	**T.W. Dreaper**	**P. Taaffe**

GRAND ANNUAL CHASE

1946	Loyal King	C. A. Rogers	D.L. Moore
1958	Top Twenty	C. Magnier	F. Shortt
1959	Top Twenty	C. Magnier	F. Winter
1960	Mon Trois Etoiles	J. Brogan	F. Carroll

SPA HURDLE

1948	Spam	D. Rogers	A. Brabazon
1954	Lucky Dome	M. V. O'Brien	T.P. Burns
1957	Bold Baby	M. Dawson	P. Powell
1960	Solfen	W. T. O'Grady	H. Beasley
1961	Sparkling Flame	P. Sleator	H. Beasley

COUNTY HANDICAP HURDLE

1953	Teapot II	C. Magnier	P. Taaffe
1954	Bold Baby	M. Dawson	P. Powell
1958	Friendly Boy	J. Osborne	W.J. Brennan
1960	Albergo	C. Magnier	D. Page
1963	Bahrain	D. L. Moore	T. Carberry
1970	Khan	Miss D. Harty	Lord Petersham

BIRDLIP HURDLE

1955	Ahaburn	M. V. O'Brien	T.P. Burns
1958	Spring Silver	C. Magnier	H. Beasley

KIM MUIR CHASE

1946	Astrometer	C. A. Rogers	Capt.D. Baggallay
1959	Irish Coffee	C. McCartan	Mr.G. Kindersley

NATIONAL HUNT HANDICAP CHASE

1946	Dungshaughlin	C. A. Rogers	R.J. O'Ryan
1952	Royal Tan	M. V. O'Brien	Mr.A.S. O'Brien
1954	Quare Times	M. V. O'Brien	P. Taaffe
1957	**Sentina**	**T. W. Dreaper**	**P. Taaffe**
1958	**Sentina**	**T. W. Dreaper**	**P. Taaffe**
1966	**Arkloin**	**T. W. Dreaper**	**P. Taaffe**

SUN ALLIANCE CHASE
(Formerly Broadway and Tote Novice Chase)

1953	Coneyburrow	J. Osborne	P. Taaffe
1955	Great Eliza	D. Morgan	B. Cooper
1960	Solfen	W. T. O'Grady	P. Taaffe
1961	Grallagh Cnoc	J. Osborne	P. Taaffe
1963	**Arkle**	**T. W. Dreaper**	**P. Taaffe**
1965	**Arkloin**	**T. W. Dreaper**	**L. McLoughlin**
1968	Herring Gull	P. Mullins	J. Crowley
1970	**Proud Tarquin**	**T. W. Dreaper**	**P. Taaffe**

ARKLE CHALLENGE TROPHY CHASE
(Formerly Cotswold Chase)

1958	**Fortria**	**T. W. Dreaper**	**T. Taaffe**
1961	**Mountcashel King**	**T. W. Dreaper**	**P. Taaffe**
1963	**Ben Stack**	**T. W. Dreaper**	**P. Taaffe**
1965	**Flyingbolt**	**T. W. Dreaper**	**P. Taaffe**
1967	Arctic Stream	P. Rooney	B. Hannon
1971	**Alpheus**	**T. W. Dreaper**	**E. Wright**

Totals 1946 - 1971

All Irish trainers = 94

Tom Dreaper = 26

Vincent O'Brien = 22

Dan Moore = 10
(plus 4 after 1971)

Leap Frog ridden by Val O'Brien wins the Wills Premier Chase at Haydock in January 1971. He went on to win the Massey Ferguson Chase at Cheltenham in November 1971 to give Tom his last winner there with his last runner. Tom's first runner at Cheltenham had also been a winner when Prince Regent won the Gold Cup in 1946. Leap Frog was originally a Kilcooley horse.

Kilcooley Abbey in Tipperary, the home of George and Libby Ponsonby, was a constant supply of wonderful young horses many of whom were to win top class races for the Greenogue stable.

The Ponsonby's, like the Dreaper's, were keen hunting people. The two couples used to select yearlings at Goff's sales. The yearlings then went down to Kilcooley for two or three years before they went into training with Tom.

Ned Barniville was responsible for some 50 years, at Kilcooley, for the young horses. He used to break them and teach them to jump loose in school with great skill.

Above, Leap Frog being broken as a two year old.
Right, Arkloin as a yearling.

The drive up to Kilcooley Abbey.

Tom, George and his two spaniels, Fan and Meg

Stonehaven as a three year old.

Garrynagree as a three year old.

Flyingbolt as a yearling.

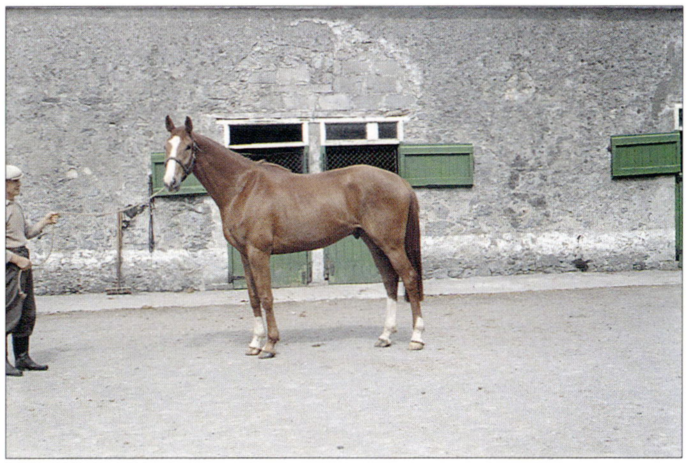

Flyingbolt as a three year old

The Duchess' Scrapbook

After this picture, the Duchess sent Tom and Betty a card asking them why they taught their horses to cross their paws?

Three leading ladies from the National Hunt world on the Duchess' Scottish Estate.
Left to right: Nora Pearson, the mother-in-law of Fred Winter and grandmother of Jim Wilson, who both rode Cheltenham Gold Cup winners.
The Duchess, who has owned some of the great steeplechasers of all time, and Betty who has been involved in the training of two of the immortals, Prince Regent and Arkle.

The Duchess' Scrapbook

The Duchess is recognised to be a wonderful judge of young chasers, but what I have noticed is her great affinity to all animals. The pictures of the Duchess and Arkle were taken when he was summering at her Bryanstown Stud.

Tom and Betty with their dog, their three children, and a borrowed child on a family holiday in Donegal in 1955.

Valerie plays with Sputnik in the late 1960s, Sputnik was Tom's favourite dog although given to Jim by Tom's brother, Dick.

Pat, Harry Bonner, Joe Osborne, Connie Mellon, Tom, Betty and Dick Mellon in the paddock.

The Dreaper Scrapbook

Tom talks to Her Majesty, The Queen Mother, whilst in the background Betty talks to Col. Stephen Hall-Dillon and Elizabeth Thomson at Cheltenham in the 1960's.

Tom goes for a camel ride, while on a not too particularly successful holiday in Morocco in 1973.

Tom was wonderful company and greatly enjoyed small parties with close friends.

Index to photograph captions